Cows

Remember Me Series

By

Caroline Norsk

Remember me I am a cow.

Remember me I eat grass most of the time.

Remember me I cannot see the colors red and green.

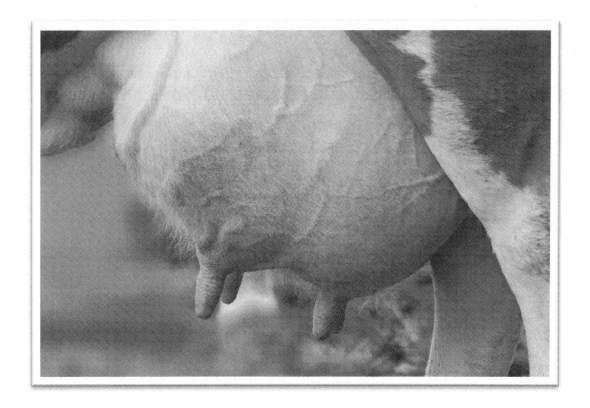

Remember me I give humans meat and milk.

Remember me we can only produce milk after we give birth to a calf.

Remember me I can be milked for three to four years.

Remember me it takes me eight hours a day to completely chew my food.

Remember me we provide almost 90% of milk in the world.

Remember me I have 32 teeth.

Remember me I choose my friends well – I stay close with three to four cows at a time.

Remember me I can be angry sometimes and avoid those cows that made me feel that way.

Remember me I produce more milk if I receive nice and proper treatment.

Remember me I love to solve problems on my own.

Remember me I show my excitement when I am allowed to go outside after staying inside for a long time.

Remember me the color red does not really make me angry – I can't see red, remember?

Remember me I only sleep for four hours a day.

Remember me I can climb up the stairs but I can't climb back down.

Remember me cows can be pregnant for nine months – just like humans do.

Remember me we can live for more than 20 years.

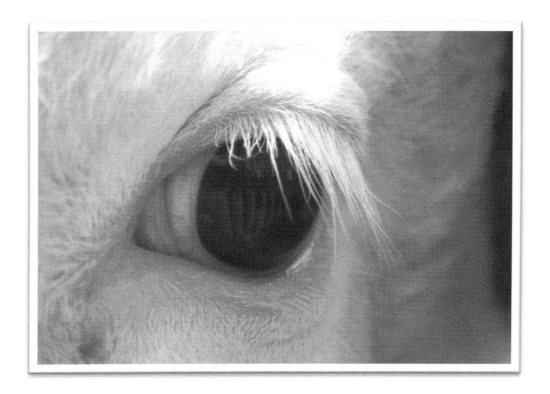

Remember me you can guess a cow's age by counting the rings on its horns – if it has any.

Thank you.

Good Luck.

74990864R00016

Made in the USA
San Bernardino, CA
23 April 2018